The Second Chester Book of Motets

The English School for 4 voices

Edited by Anthony G. Pe

GW00536160

LIST OF MOTETS

		Page
William Byrd	*Ave Verum*	2
William Byrd	*Cibavit Eos*	6
William Byrd	*Senex Puerum*	10
William Byrd	*Venite Comedite*	13
Robert Johnson	*Dum Transisset*	16
Thomas Morley	*Agnus Dei*	20
John Shepherd	*In Manus Tuas*	22
Thomas Tallis	*Euge Caeli*	25
Thomas Tallis	*Sancte Deus*	27
John Taverner	*Alleluia*	33
John Taverner	*Audivi*	35
Christopher Tye	*Gloria Laus*	38
Editor's notes		42

Chester Music
(A Music Sales Limited Company)
8/9 Frith Street, London, W1V 5TZ

Cover:
Virgin and Child in a landscape. Netherlandish School.
Presented by Queen Victoria to the National Gallery
at the Prince Consort's wish in 1863
Reproduced by courtesy of the Trustees,
The National Gallery, London.

AVE VERUM

Hail to the true body, born of the Virgin Mary, which truly suffered on the cross for mankind; and from whose side water flowed with the blood. Grant that we may taste you at the hour of our death. O sweet, loving son of Mary, have mercy on me.

William Byrd (1543 – 1623)

CIBAVIT EOS

He fed them from the fulness of the wheat and sated them with honey from the rock.
Alleluia. Rejoice in God our helper, sing for joy to the God of Jacob. Glory be to
the Father, the Son, and the Holy Spirit, as it was in the beginning, is now, and
ever shall be. Amen (*Ps. lxxx,* 17.)

William Byrd (1543 – 1623)

SENEX PUERUM

The old man carried the child, but the child was the old man's King. A
virgin gave birth to that child, yet remained a virgin: the one she bore
she also adored.

William Byrd (1543 – 1623)

VENITE COMEDITE

Come and eat my bread and drink the wine which I have prepared for you.

William Byrd (1543 – 1623)

14

DUM TRANSISSET

When the sabbath came, Mary Magdalen, Mary the mother of James, and
Salome bought spices for anointing Jesus. Alleluia (*Mark,* xvi, 1.)

Robert Johnson (early 16th cent.)

AGNUS DEI

Lamb of God, who takes away the sin of the world, have mercy on us.

Thomas Morley (1557 – 1603)

IN MANUS TUAS

Into your hands, Lord, I commend my spirit. You have redeemed us, O Lord,
God of truth.

John Shepherd (c. 1515 – c. 1560)

EUGE CAELI

Rejoice Gate of Heaven, for now you are open, you have let into the world
the Light of Truth, the Sun of Justice himself, clothed in flesh.

Thomas Tallis (c. 1505 – 1585)

SANCTE DEUS

Holy God, Strong, Holy and Immortal One, have mercy on us. Now, O
Christ, we beseech you and beg you to have mercy on us. You came to
redeem the lost: do not condemn those whom you saved; for by your
cross you have redeemed the world. Amen.

Thomas Tallis (c. 1505 – 1585)

30

32

ALLELUIA

John Taverner (c. 1495 – 1545)

34

AUDIVI

I heard: there was a cry at midnight: see, the bridegroom is coming.

John Taverner (c. 1495 – 1545)

36

GLORIA LAUS

Glory, praise and honour to you, Redeemer King, to whom the children sang their glad hosannas. You are the King of Israel, of David's royal lineage: a blessed king, you come in the name of the Lord. The Hebrew people went out to meet you with palms: see how we greet you with prayers, vows and hymns.

Christopher Tye (c. 1500 – 1573)

EDITOR'S NOTES

While the madrigal is now coming into its own in terms of individual editions and collections, the motet is still somewhat neglected, and has even suffered a setback, because the disappearance of Latin from the Roman Catholic liturgy has caused many works to go out of print. Musicologists continue to introduce new editions, but their main emphasis is on the provision of larger scale works for the concert hall, or of scholarly editions which are often beyond the scope of the average choir to decipher and transpose, let alone sing.

The aim of the present series is to make more readily available a comprehensive body of Latin motets from the Renaissance period, combining old favourites with lesser known or hitherto unpublished works. The first five volumes are arranged nationally, covering Italy, England, Spain, Germany and Slavic areas, and the Low Countries; each contains, on average, twelve motets drawn from not less than six composers. They are for four mixed voices, and should all be within the scope of the reasonably able choir. They also provide a fair selection from the liturgical year, as a guide for the church choir and for performing choirs who like to present their music according to theme or season.

The editor has endeavoured to preserve a balance between a critical and a performing edition. The motets are transposed into the most practical performing keys, are barred, fully underlayed, provided with breathing marks, and have a reduction as a rehearsal aid. Editorial tempi and dynamics are also supplied, but only in the reduction, leaving choirmasters free to select their own in the light of their interpretation of a given piece, vocal resources and the acoustics. The vocal range for all parts is given at the beginning of each motet.

As an aid to musicologists, the motets, wherever possible, are transcribed from the most authoritative source, and the original clefs, signatures and note values are given at the beginning and wherever they change during the course of a piece. Ligatures are indicated by slurs, editorial accidentals are placed above the stave, and the underlay is shown in italics when it expands a ditto sign, or in square brackets when entirely editorial.

Each volume includes a brief introduction concerning the scope of the edition, with notes on the composers, the motets, the sources, editorial emendations and alterations, if any, and a table of use according to the Tridentine Rite.

Assembling a volume of Renaissance SATB motets by English composers poses certain difficulties. First of all, with the establishment of an English liturgy in the reign of Edward VI, the use of Latin in church music rapidly declined. The process was temporarily halted with the accession of Mary Tudor, but was so fully implemented by the later years of Elizabeth's reign as to make the use or even the publication of Latin church music a rarity, with a few notable exceptions, including the works of William Byrd, though there was a gap in the publication of even his Latin works in the last decade of Elizabeth's reign. By the early 17th century, the only other English composers still writing Latin liturgical music in any quantity were the Catholic exiles like Peter Philips and Richard Deering.

A further difficulty is that in the late 16th century four-part writing was relatively uncommon among English composers of Church Music, who favoured five or more voices, or, especially in the early baroque period, one, two or three voices with organ continuo. So it is that such composers as Philips and Deering are not represented and that the collection relies heavily, though securely, on Byrd. In the earlier 16th century, four-part compositions are more common, but here there is the problem of obtaining a suitable SATB range, because many of the works are for equal voices, while in most of the others the tenor and alto lines constantly overlap, in many cases making both parts comfortable only for counter-tenors. It has therefore been necessary to switch the two parts occasionally in a few bars, as noted below, to accommodate them more readily to a mixed-voices setting. In the works of Early Tudor composers especially, there is often the further problem of rhythmical intricacies which may be beyond the scope of all but the most professional and sophisticated choir. Notwithstanding these limitations, it has been found possible to include motets from virtually all the major 16th century English composers of Latin motets, as well as from one or two lesser known ones. William Byrd fittingly leads off the collection, because in addition to being alphabetically first, he is also the most copious and, by general consent, the greatest composer of the English Renaissance. Among the many remarkable things about Byrd is the freedom with which he was permitted not only to write but to publish so much Latin church music of the Roman Rite, and in fact was given a monopoly of music printing. That he was given so much latitude is a strong indication of how highly he was esteemed by the Queen, who although a great patroness of the arts, nevertheless gave ready assent to ever-mounting anti-Catholic legislation. He was even for a time organist of the Chapel Royal, holding the initial appointment jointly with his teacher and close friend, Thomas Tallis. Neither does Byrd seem to have surrendered his Catholicism, for he was frequently cited as a recusant, and he seems to have given liberally of his friendship and aid to missionary priests, including Robert Southwell and Henry Garnet. His closeness to the spirituality of the Roman liturgy is reflected throughout all his Latin music, motets and masses alike, though he was also a pioneer in the shaping of the tradition of Anglican Church music. Coupled with Byrd's copiousness and musical integrity is his great sense of variety and imagination, for he repeats himself remarkably infrequently and can respond to virtually any liturgical text. His versatility and inventiveness, wedded to economy of means, are clearly to be seen in the four pieces included here. The first three are taken from *Gradualia ac Cantiones Sacrae, Liber Primus*, 1605, reprinted 1610, which includes twenty four-part motets. Of these the best known is the *Ave Verum*, a masterpiece of apparent simplicity, set homophonically almost throughout, at a gently moving pace so that the full meditative effect of the words is conveyed. The speech rhythms are not only followed but inventively explored, with subtle and restrained syncopation for key words and phrases (*e.g.* "immolatum", "perforatum", "fluxit"). An especially notable feature is the repetition of the section from "O dulcis". The handling of the triple invocation is partly inspired by the plainsong, especially in the gradually mounting tension as the voices move up to "O Jesu". The supplication "miserere mei", which follows is possibly a personal touch, because there is no equivalent in the liturgical text, and conveys a very wistful yearning, especially in the opening duet, and in the false relations between G and G♯. The motet then comes quietly to rest with the undulation of the lower parts in the optimistic "Amen". Particularly effective, too, in the piece are the striking modulations and the generally careful alternation of A major and minor, though there is still the feeling of the Aeolian mode. The *Ave Verum* and the next work, *Cibavit Eos*, are both motets in honour of the Blessed Sacrament, but in other respects are very different. The *Cibavit Eos*, in the Mixolydian mode, is very buoyant, with a bustling movement, and is especially ebullient in the *Verse* section, "Exsultate Deo". Three styles are basically used: a quasi-polyphonic or "mixed" style for the opening, with some verbal repetition and a syncopated and fairly melismatic set of alleluias. The *Verse* lightens the texture by dropping the bass line and using an open and breezy fugal style with quite intricate turns on the cadence for "Jacob", and then moves into the monosyllabic and homophonic beginning of the doxology before fanning out into a quite extended and sequential "saeculorum. Amen" to depict the eternal praise of the Trinity. It should be noted that for strict liturgical use as an Introit it would have been necessary to repeat the whole of the first section (bars 1-29), but the motet makes good musical sense and ends quite effectively without this repetition.

Senex Puerum, the third Byrd motet, one of two settings, the other being for five voices, is a tender and unobtrusive motet with a quiet beauty which grows on the ear with repetition. Though it begins apparently in formal style with a well-spaced fugue at the fifth moving down the parts in an orderly progression, it is somewhat unusual in having such a marked descent in each part and then a sudden leap of a minor sixth in the two upper parts, and an octave in the two lower ones, apparently emphasizing the contrast between the old man and his boy king. There follows a touch of word-painting on the gently rocking melisma for the stressed syllable of "portabat" and a strong ending of the first section with all parts together for "regebat". The next section, "quem Virgo" begins appropriately with a lighter texture in duets of close harmony, but gathers momentum as all parts participate for "ipsum quem genuit", and ends in a quite florid rising sequence for the climactic "adoravit".

The final Byrd piece, taken from *Gradualia ac Cantiones Sacrae, Liber Secundus* (1607, reprinted 1610) is the much overlooked *Venite Comedite* (the second part of *Ab ortu solis*), which for its delicacy, emotive power and variety can hold its own with almost any of Byrd's four-part motets, including the others to the Blessed Sacrament, a feast for which Byrd seems to have expressed a particularly strong musical devotion. Alternating the Mixolydian mode for mystical joy with the Ionian (or A major) for bright exultation, Byrd uses a quasi-fugal and free style so that each liturgical phrase seems to have its separate identity. The opening invocation begins slowly and sweetly, with the tenor and alto moving in thirds, even in a fourth leap. It is then intensified by the addition of the bass, and by the soprano taking over the tenor phrase, while the tenor moves in sixths with it. With "comedite" there is a sprightlier rhythm in fugal style. A chain of duets follow for "et bibite vinum", moving into an exquisite trio of upper voices with its succession of 6/3 chords (bars 23-4). The final section, "quod miscui vobis" becomes increasingly expansive and reassuring.

The next composer, Robert Johnson (c. 1490-c.1560), not to be confused with the Jacobean composer of that name, was a Scottish priest who fled to England in the reign of Henry VIII to escape a charge of heresy. Relatively little of his music has survived, it being fairly equally divided between that for the Anglican service and Latin motets. His works are scattered through manuscript part-books of the 16th century, the present piece, *Dum transisset* being one of three settings in the Gyffard part-books (British Library, Additional MSS. 17802-5), the others being by Robert Barber and John Taverner. The Johnson setting seems to have been somewhat influenced by the Taverner, not only in the use of plainsong melody *cantus firmus* (in the baritone in the five-part Taverner) but in some of the melodic phrasing, as in "aromata". The motet is, in fact, in more traditional style than is usually associated with Johnson, though it certainly has greater melodic smoothness and less unprepared dissonance than is common in Early Tudor polyphony. Among the notable features of the piece is its fine sense of integration and the way in which the gentle melodic curves of the other three lines match the plainsong of the tenor. Above all, it establishes from the very outset a mood depicting the gradual and not fully realised dawning of Easter, so that even the final alleluias, though at a quickened pace, convey a quiet rather than a boisterous joy.

Thomas Morley (1557-1603) is best known for his madrigals, and his sacred music forms only a small fraction of his total output. Barely ten complete motets are known to survive, two of them, including the *Agnus Dei*, being published as examples at the back of his *Plain and Easy introduction to Practical Music* (1597, reprinted 1608). The text is not strictly liturgical, ending with "miserere nostri" rather than "miserere nobis" and without any provision for "dona nobis pacem", and so is obviously an isolated piece rather than part of a Mass. It is a very unusual work, difficult to fathom stylistically, and with somewhat unpredictable progressions and cadences. Contributing to this unusual effect is the way in which the Dorian mode is constantly modified by the use of D♭, giving the impression of the Aeolian mode; but then this resultant minor tonality is constantly offset by quite frequent actual or implied major cadences. Echoes of other sacred works can be found in the piece, most notably the *Angus Dei* sections of Byrd's *Mass for Five Voices*, and possibly touches of Early Baroque Italian composers, including Felice Anerio. The opening phrase moves chiefly by step up to "Dei", somewhat in the style of Byrd. The main melismas are reserved for "mundi", though the tenor, both in the opening and throughout the piece, has a roving commission of ornamentation. Then, balancing the opening ascent are the frequently repeated descending passages for "miserere nostri", again similar to those in Byrd, using pairs and trios to give the impression of waves of supplication. The final phrase, with the three upper parts coming to rest against the held bass note has something of an Italian flavour. All in all, the piece has an elusive and disturbing beauty, and makes a remarkable impact in a surprisingly brief span.

The next composer, John Shepherd or Sheppard, is one of the most prolific composers of the mid-Tudor period and, like most of his contemporaries (whether from conviction or expediency) wrote liturgical music in both English and Latin. What little is known of his life is unsavoury in places, and he is most remembered for his sadistic treatment of choir boys under his charge at Magdalen College, Oxford, one of whom he is said to have dragged in chains from Malmesbury. Among his fifty or more motets are several responsories, including *In Manus Tuas* (British Library, Additional MSS. 17802-5), in which, traditionally, plainsong alternated with polyphony, a common practice with Shepherd and called an *alternatim* setting. The plainsong has been inserted here editorially from the Sarum Rite, and, strictly speaking, the section of it from "commendo" to the end should follow at the end of the polyphony. It would also have been normal, except in Passiontide, to sing the plainsong *Gloria Patri* at the end, after which the first section, "In manus" and the plainsong which follows it would have been repeated. Before Shepherd's time, the plainsong was sung in unison by the whole choir and the polyphony by soloists, but the practice was later reversed, with the plainsong sung by a soloist or cantors, and the polyphony by the whole choir, a method recommended for this motet. The style is remarkably accomplished. The tranquil optimism of the piece is conveyed by consistently major tonality passing through a number of bright modes from the initial Ionian through a form of transposed Ionian (bar 12) to the dominant cadence of an implied E major tonic in yet another transposed Ionian mode, though part of the reason for this is the necessity of moving into a suitable cadence to accommodate the ensuing plainsong. The texture is appropriately layered, each polyphonic section beginning in the lower voices and making its way by fugue calmly and hopefully to the crowning melody of the top line. The final passages for "Deus veritatis" have an almost jaunty movement, all parts coming more closely together for the last affirmation of the text (bar 32), the three upper parts moving towards the final cadence with a highly emotive falling run of 6/3 chords (bar 35).

Thomas Tallis (c. 1505-1585) is one of the trinity of T's among Tudor composers (the others being Taverner and Tye), and his long career extends from the late Henrician period until well into the middle years of Elizabeth's reign. In stature among Church composers he is second only to William Byrd, whose teacher he was, and with whom he was on terms of closest friendship. Apart from being organists of the Chapel Royal they also jointly produced the celebrated *Cantiones Sacrae* of 1575. Tallis seems equally at home in the Latin and English Rite, and his works are generally typified by a uniform warmth and grandeur of design, whether in a relatively simple piece like "*If Ye Love Me*" or the magnificent forty-part *Spem in Alium*. *Euge Caeli* (St. Michael's, Tenbury, MSS. 354-8), a setting of the second verse of the sequence to the Virgin, *Ave Praeclara*, is a very tender piece with many haunting phrases, for all its brevity. While the total effect is mellifluous, it is to be noted that Tallis gives the piece a considerable amount of rhythmic variety, especially in the top two lines, the quick dotted rhythm of the soprano livening up the texture in a style which both looks back to the Early Tudor period and anticipates Early Baroque techniques. The *Sancte Deus* (one of two settings in British Library, Additional MSS. 17802-5) is the longest motet in the present collection and by far the most sonorous. It consists of a set of extended and powerful invocations to the Deity, beginning penitentially in extended notes in formal style, from the bottom line to the top, all phrases rising to the Deity, and then melismatically portraying the epithets, "fortis and immortalis". Each supplication ends with a fermata and a bar line. The opening of the most urgent request, "Noli damnare", begins with held notes in a style reminiscent of Josquin and of Taverner, and is followed by an intense piece of writing with all but the tenor reaching the top of their compass within the motet, though there is remarkably little reliance on dissonance, prepared or unprepared to reinforce the effect. With the "Quia per crucem" the mood becomes somewhat brighter, and the bell-like sound of the final amens seems to indicate rather more of a peal than a knell. For all the earlier sombreness of the piece, there is an overriding optimism indicated by the fact that each section ends with a major cadence, albeit sometimes after a disquieting suspension.

John Taverner (c. 1495-1545), the earliest composer in this collection, wrote a copious amount of Latin church music until he was converted to Protestantism about the middle of the reign of Henry VIII, having been accused of heresy while Master of the Children at Cardinal College (later Christ Church College), Oxford. His music is of extremely high quality, and it is unfortunate that because of their Mediaeval and Flemish intricacies in rhythm and melody, and the vocal resources employed, relatively few of his motets lend themselves to performance by even a very competent SATB choir. The first piece included here is one of a set of alleluias by various composers to be found yet again in that invaluable source of Tudor church music, Additional MSS. 17802-5. Separate polyphonic alleluias were quite common in pre-Reformation English liturgy, though in many cases they were intended as part of a Lady-Mass and were usually followed by "Ora pro nobis". They were normally based on a plainsong alleluia, as in the present case, where the plainsong in augmentation provides a form of canon for the bass, tenor and soprano while the alto moves fairly independently. The soprano maintains the plainsong as a *cantus firmus* throughout while the other parts break into melismatic scale passages for the last nine bars. The second Taverner piece, *Audivi media nocte* is, like *In manus*, another responsory, and seemingly a very popular one, since it was also set by Tallis and Shepherd among others, all three settings appearing together in Additional MSS. 17802-5. The polyphony is in three sections, and though there is no provision for it in the manuscript, it is likely that a plainsong passage is intended between the first two. For choirs wishing to include it, the Sarum version has been supplied below. The polyphony searchingly conveys the mood of the words, while maintaining the plainstong *cantus firmus*, which is carried by the soprano in the first and last sections, but passes to the alto in the middle. In the opening, all three lower parts move freely in arabesque patterns punctuated by rests in typical Taverner style. In the second section the parts are more closely knit and even occasionally paired. The last section begins with two held chords for "Ecce" (compare the "noli" of Tallis's *Sancte Deus*), and then moves excitedly into a flurry of brief figures in quick succession for "venit", culminating in a sequence of triplets, again a favourite and frequently symbolic device for Taverner.

The last of the celebrated T's, though lagging a little behind, is Christopher Tye (1500-73). In early life he was a chorister of King's College Cambridge, later becoming Master of the Choristers of Ely Cathedral (1541) and Gentleman of the Chapel Royal. He took Anglican orders in 1560. It is clear that many of Tye's works in both English and Latin have perished, and only about twenty motets are extant. Among these is *Gloria Laus* (Additional MSS. 17802-5) which is a setting of all but one verse of the Palm Sunday hymn of that name. As is customary with Tye, a *cantus firmus* is used throughout, appearing first in the tenor (to bar 30) and then in the soprano (a migrant *cantus firmus* being characteristic of Taverner, under whose influence Tye seems to have been for a while). The mode is Aeolian, in keeping with the penitential feast to which it belongs, but the specific occasion of the triumphal entry into Jerusalem